*al
e*

GUIDES

WORKING WITH
ANIMALS & WILDLIFE

REAL LIFE GUIDES

Practical guides for practical people

In this increasingly sophisticated world the need for manually skilled people to build our homes, cut our hair, fix our boilers, and to make our cars go is greater than ever. As things progress, so the level of training and competence required of our skilled manual workers increases.

In this series of career guides from Trotman, we look in detail at what it takes to train for, get into and be successful at a wide spectrum of practical careers. The *Real Life Guides* aim to inform and inspire young people and adults alike by providing comprehensive yet hard-hitting and often blunt information about what it takes to succeed in these careers.

Titles in the series are:
Real Life Guides: The Armed Forces
Real Life Guides: The Beauty Industry, 2nd edition
Real Life Guides: Care
Real Life Guides: Carpentry & Cabinet-Making, 2nd edition
Real Life Guides: Catering, 2nd edition
Real Life Guides: Construction, 2nd edition
Real Life Guides: Distribution & Logistics
Real Life Guides: Electrician, 2nd edition
Real Life Guides: The Fire Service
Real Life Guides: Hairdressing, 2nd edition
Real Life Guides: The Motor Industry, 2nd edition
Real Life Guides: Passenger Transport
Real Life Guides: Plumbing, 2nd edition
Real Life Guides: The Police Force
Real Life Guides: Retail, 2nd edition
Real Life Guides: Transport
Real Life Guides: Working Outdoors
Real Life Guides: Working with Animals & Wildlife, 2nd edition
Real Life Guides: Working with Young People

trotman

Real Life

GUIDES

WORKING WITH
ANIMALS & WILDLIFE

Brin Best &
Felicity Haynes

2nd edition

Real Life Guides: Working with Animals and Wildlife
This second edition published in 2008 by Trotman Publishing,
an imprint of Crimson Publishing Ltd, Westminster House,
Kew Road, Richmond, Surrey TW9 2ND

First edition published in 2005 by Trotman and Company Ltd

© Trotman Publishing 2008

Advertising Sarah Talbot, Advertising Sales Director;
Kerry Lyon, Senior Account Manager

Design by XAB

British Library Cataloguing in Publications Data
A catalogue record for this book is available
from the British Library

ISBN 978 1 84455 152 1

Typeset by Ellipsis Books Ltd, Glasgow
Printed and bound in the UK at MPG Books Ltd, Bodmin

A0056780
#9-99
20/05/2008

636

About the authors

Brin Best is the Director of Innovation *for* Education Ltd, an education training and consultancy company based in Yorkshire. He has a degree in environmental sciences and is a qualified teacher. Prior to his work as a teacher and education adviser, he worked in wildlife conservation as a marine ornithologist and tropical rainforest researcher. Brin has written or edited 16 other books on topics ranging from tropical forest ecology to the wildlife of the Yorkshire Dales. He is very active as a volunteer within wildlife organisations, and is a trustee of the Royal Society for the Protection of Birds.

Felicity Haynes lives in the Yorkshire Dales and has been involved with animals and animal care all her life. Felicity has a degree in geography and health studies and is currently working part-time in a school as a teaching assistant, as well as writing on a freelance basis. Her main passion is horses, and she is a regular competitor in riding competitions. She enjoys driving her pony around the quiet lanes of the Yorkshire Dales in a two-wheeled cart, and keeps a variety of pets including dogs, cats and guinea pigs. Felicity is keen to inspire young people to pursue a career working with animals and wildlife.

Acknowledgements

We are very grateful to all those people who agreed to be interviewed for this book – their support made the project possible and enriched the text considerably. We would like to thank Anne Harley, director of human resources at the Royal Society for the Protection of Birds (RSPB), who provided valuable comments that helped us improve the book. Anne also put us in touch with Sally Mills, site manager at Ham Wall RSPB reserve. Gill O'Donnell and Rosie Haynes provided helpful comments on an earlier draft of this book and Mina Patria and Rachel Lockhart provided valuable editorial support in the Trotman office.

Foreword

The UK is well known for being a nation of animal lovers. However, this is not just a UK trait: 64% of the world's population owns a pet. This has led to many businesses devoted to providing care for our animals; for example, dog grooming parlours, pet stores, kennels and catteries, pet rescue centres and zoos.

It is a common belief that one of the hardest careers is working with animals. City & Guilds NPTC have developed a large range of qualifications in animal care to provide the knowledge to deal with these jobs. These qualifications are suitable for anyone who has an interest in the area or is planning a career in animal care or welfare. We offer a range of NVQs in Animal Care from levels 1 to 3; we also offer level 2 National Certificate, and level 3 Advanced National Certificate and Advanced National Diploma in Animal Care.

These qualifications cover a range of issues concerned with animal care such as animal housing, animal behaviour, animal health, pet retail operations, breeding, dog grooming and animal training amongst others.

We also offer two qualifications in dog grooming, the level 2 Intermediate Certificate in Dog Grooming and the level 3 Advanced Certificate in Dog Grooming for learners specifically interested in grooming parlours.

City & Guilds NPTC prides itself on the fact that qualifications are developed with leading industry experts, such as the Pet Care Trust, to ensure that the qualifications are fit for purpose, at the highest possible standards and most suited to the industry and the demand and needs within it.

If a career in animal care interests you then why not visit our websites for more details:

www.cityandguilds.com or www.nptc.org.uk.

City & Guilds are delighted to be part of the Trotman *Real Life Guides* series to help raise awareness of these vocational qualifications. If the idea of working with animals and wildlife appeals to you then City & Guilds has qualifications which will support development throughout your career, helping you to achieve excellence and quality in whatever field you choose.

Introduction

What images come to mind when you think about working with animals?

- Carrying out lifesaving operations on sick animals?
- Training guide dogs to help transform the lives of blind people?
- Protecting endangered birds on pristine nature reserves?
- Helping to run a small organic farm?

Working with animals and wildlife certainly offers a wide range of exciting and rewarding opportunities: this book will help you consider them in detail.

You are probably reading this because you already have an interest in animals or wildlife and want to know more about how you can make it into a career. If so, you have come to the right place, as this book is designed to help you make sensible choices about the next steps you can take.

The employment sector linked to working with animals and wildlife is currently booming, so there has never been a better time to enter the sector.

IT'S NOT ALL CUDDLY ANIMALS AND LONG DAYS IN THE SUN

Working with animals and wildlife can be very rewarding, but before you read any further you need to be aware that

DID YOU KNOW?

1.5 million people work in the environmental and land-based sector in the UK, and over 25,000 new people will be needed in the next five years.

it also has its fair share of challenges. Long hours, dirt, sweat, blood and tears ... all are guaranteed at some point in the job. Because of this, a key point to bear in mind is that you must be really determined if you want to pursue a career working in this sector. You also need to really care about animals and wildlife without being too sentimental about them, and this can be a difficult balance to achieve.

Having said that, the rewards are certainly there if you can rise to the challenge. You could find yourself seeing wounded animals through to a successful recovery, working in spectacular scenery with exotic wildlife in the Ecuadorian rainforests or feeling incredibly proud when a horse that you have spent months training wins a show-jumping competition.

You need to really care about animals and wildlife without being too sentimental about them, and this can be a difficult balance to achieve.

WHAT TYPES OF JOBS ARE ON OFFER?

There are six main categories of work with animals and wildlife:

- **Animal health and welfare** – including occupations such as physiotherapist, vet, animal behaviourist, dog warden, alternative therapist and animal technician

- **Animal care charities** – including work at rescue centres and/or for organisations such as the Royal Society for the Prevention of Cruelty to Animals (RSPCA)
- **Wildlife management and conservation** – including work to protect species or habitats for charities such as the Royal Society for the Protection of Birds (RSPB) in jobs such as farm wildlife adviser, fisheries scientist, ecologist, scientific researcher and gamekeeper
- **The animal and wildlife business** – including jobs such as farmer, fish-farmer, auctioneer, riding instructor, falconer, river bailiff or animal breeder/trainer in locations such as horse studs, kennels and catteries, zoos and the countryside. This area also includes wildlife entertainment and tourism
- **Services provided through animals** – including work as a dog handler for the police, customs or the mounted police
- **Indirect animal and wildlife occupations** – including animal nutrition, working in a pet food shop, tack shop or feed merchants or educating people about animals and wildlife.

Each of these categories is explored in more detail in Chapter 4. This book will focus most on those professions that have direct contact with animals and wildlife, thereby touching only briefly on the last category. We will also stay clear of those jobs involving animals that are not alive (eg taxidermist, pest control officer, slaughterhouse worker etc).

WHO CAN YOU WORK FOR?
One of the advantages of a career working with animals or wildlife is that it is possible to find employment in a huge

range of different situations. As shown by the list of job types on the previous page, it is possible to work for employers as diverse as:

- Government agencies such as the Environment Agency or Natural England
- National or local charities, such as the RSPCA and the county wildlife trusts
- Private companies or individuals providing relevant products and services
- Yourself (ie being self-employed).

The kind of work you undertake within these different sectors can be radically different too, and many of the jobs give you the chance to work with other colleagues and with the general public. Whatever type of job you focus on, you are sure to develop a wide range of useful skills along the way, which will be transferable to other careers.

It is also worth noting that some of the jobs listed above are quite competitive and some need very specific qualifications. For example, a lot of young people are interested in marine biology or veterinary science, but not everyone can get the A level grades needed to study these subjects at university. Make sure you are realistic about what you can achieve.

WHERE CAN YOU WORK?

You will be pleased to hear that for many of the jobs that involve working with animals or wildlife you can more or less take your pick of where to live and work. There are opportunities in every part of the UK, in built-up as well as rural areas.

Even if you choose a career in wildlife conservation, you should not rule out getting a job in a city. Many of our best nature reserves are now located in urban areas – for example, the award-winning London Wetland Centre, which protects over 40 hectares of specially created wetland in the heart of London. Although only established in 2000, this Wildfowl and Wetlands Trust reserve is already a Site of Special Scientific Interest (SSSI), supporting nationally important numbers of ducks.

DID YOU KNOW?

The National Trust is the largest single private landowner in the UK.

Of course many people working with animals or wildlife love the wild outdoors too. Working in this sector will certainly give you the chance to live and work in some of the most outstanding natural areas of the UK, or even overseas.

HOW THIS BOOK WILL HELP

This book will guide you through the various career routes to consider if you are thinking of working with animals or wildlife. It will also give you the chance to think more deeply about whether this really is a job area for you.

Throughout the book there are in-depth interviews with people who already work with animals and wildlife in the 'Case Studies' and 'Real Lives' chapters. Like you, at some point in their lives the people interviewed in this book felt the desire to seriously consider this career option, and those featured stuck with it and now get paid to work with animals and wildlife.

We firmly believe that you can learn a huge amount by talking to those who are out there doing the work, and we hope the interviews and case studies in this book will help you build up a more comprehensive picture of what daily life is like working with animals and wildlife. Below is a list of interviews featured in this book:

We have also included a quiz to help you gauge how much you already know about animals and wildlife. At the end of the book is a further information section which will show you where to go to find out more.

TIME FOR REFLECTION
It is a good idea to pause at this stage and consider a few important questions that will help you get the most out of this book:

- What do you already know about careers with animals and wildlife? (You can use the quiz on page 48 to test yourself on this.)
- What specifically do you want to find out from this book?
- Which types of jobs, if any, have you already considered?

The key message we want to put across is that the best thing you can do to ensure that you are making the right choice is to carry out plenty of research before taking any major steps. This book will help you to begin this process.

Success stories

PAT O'BRIEN

After taking his A levels at the Leeds school where the Kaiser Chiefs were educated, Pat O'Brien was fed up with his academic studies and did not feel inspired to progress on to university. Instead, he longed for a career working outdoors and soon joined Yorkshire Water as a scientific and technical assistant. As we will see from this interview, this lack of 'academic' qualifications did not stop him progressing into a key fisheries management role with the Environment Agency.

When did you first become interested in wildlife?

Birth! I was an inquisitive child fascinated with wildlife. I was brought up in a rural area, so spent much time in the countryside. My father was a keen gardener, so I used to earn my pocket money helping in the garden.

Whilst qualifications are important, what really matters to an employer is a proven track record of achievements and honest enthusiasm and flexibility to work in a team.

This exposed me to the wide range of insects that are often regarded as pests. At one point I used to keep and breed butterflies. I also used to accompany my father shooting and fishing, although never really embraced the former.

What is your current job and how did you end up there?
My current job title is Fisheries and Recreation Technical Team Leader for the Environment Agency. I began working for Yorkshire Water straight after leaving school when I was 18 in a role linked to fisheries and biological sciences – this was for four years. I then progressed to become a Fisheries Inspector for the National Rivers Authority where I spent another eight years, before taking on management duties as a Senior Fisheries Inspector for five years. I was then promoted to my current role, which has a greater focus on leadership, which I have been doing for ten years.

What does a fisheries inspector do?
You are very much the public face of the Environment Agency for all those people who have an interest in fish. You are responsible for a particular stretch of a river or for several rivers, and work with landowners, fishermen, fish farmers and other people who would like to see improvements in the river. Quite a lot of survey work is also carried out. Some of this involves 'electro-fishing' for which you need to wear some specialist equipment including chest-high rubber wading boots. The technique is done by putting an electrified probe into the water which forces fish to swim in a way that makes them easy to catch in a hand net. Once caught, the fish are measured and scale samples taken before being returned unharmed to the river. The role also involves work with schools, which can be very rewarding.

What are the main aspects of your current role?
I now have to inspire people in my team, be a role model for work in this field and have a very clear vision of where we are going as a team – this is very much the realm of leadership. There are also management tasks, such as deciding on work plans and priorities and running things on a day-to-day basis. It is a varied and demanding role.

You are very much the public face of the Environment Agency for all those people who have an interest in fish.

What species do you work with?
Not surprisingly, I work mostly with fish in my current job. Many of the projects I have managed, however, have improved the environment for all wildlife.

What made you progress into management/leadership?
I got frustrated with how things were being managed and wanted to play my part in making things better. I figured that the only real way to make changes was to become a manager. During my early career, a lot of my own time was taken up with bringing up a family. This delayed some of the professional training I undertook to a time when my children were less demanding.

Did you consider any other jobs?
My early career aim in life was quite simple. I wanted to work outdoors, in the countryside. I considered going into agriculture or horticulture. I also considered becoming a fish farmer, gamekeeper, dry-stone waller and even a vet.

What hours do you work in an average week?
I am paid to work 37 hours a week, but a typical week is usually about 50 hours as I often work early in the morning, evenings and weekends, so I work unpaid for about 13 hours every week.

I am paid to work 37 hours a week, but a typical week is usually about 50 hours.

What training to do you have?
After leaving school with A levels, I could not face the prospect of further education so started work at 18. I was then fortunate to be allowed day release at local colleges gaining additional diplomas in scientific subjects, although back in the 1980s there were very few environmental science options available. I have thus been training ever since 'on the job' and have the Institute of Fisheries Management (IFM) Certificate and Diploma. I am also a Chartered Environmentalist for the Society for the Environment (Soc-En).

What are the highs and lows of the job?
The highs are when you get positive praise for having helped an angling club make their fishery better. I have also really enjoyed creating new fisheries and helping deprived groups to enjoy and take ownership of their own local environment. The lows are the hoops one has to jump through to obtain funding for a project. It is also frustrating that not everyone shares my passion for my job and that my employer sometimes has different priorities to my own. This is often a challenge with a larger employer.

What changes have you seen during your 25 years working on Yorkshire rivers?

It is great to see so many fish species coming back to Yorkshire's rivers, even those rivers that run through built-up areas. This has been a result of an improvement in sewage treatment, better controls on industry and more careful farming practices. Fish such as salmon, brown trout and even grayling can now be found on many rivers in the region I work in. The increase in fish is a sign that water quality is improving and this is having knock-on benefits for other wildlife. Birds such as herons, kingfishers and goosanders (which all eat fish) are becoming regular sights on our rivers and there have even been reports of otters locally.

What plans do you have for the future?

As a team leader, I achieve most by enabling a team to deliver the same work I used to do myself. I aim to retain a high performing team and to assist in their development. I will continue to identify efficient working and guide my team to deliver projects where greatest gains can be made to the environment for wildlife and people.

Above all make sure you learn from your experience and remember that persistence really pays.

What advice would you give somebody interested in pursuing a career in this field?

Do not be daunted by academic requirements. It has not hindered me in progressing to a senior level in my organisation and the barriers are more in your mind than a reality. Whilst qualifications are important, what really matters to an employer is a proven track record of achievements and honest enthusiasm and flexibility to work in a team. Make early decisions on what wildlife career you want to get, find out what jobs are available, the employing organisations, then make an appointment to go and talk to the manager. You may only get a 15 minute slot, but this will be invaluable in setting your targets on getting the job you really want. The next stage is being realistic about often limited opportunities in the environmental field, and realising that you will have to make compromises, which may mean working in another part of the country. If you are really keen to get involved in hands-on conservation work, then working for one of the government agencies could be rather frustrating, as there is also a lot of administration work to do – this has increased in recent years as government regulation has grown. Above all make sure you learn from your experience and remember that persistence really pays.

STEVE LEONARD

Steve Leonard is a veterinary surgeon and a well-known television wildlife presenter. He works with dogs, cats and rabbits in his veterinary surgery in the UK and also travels the world making documentaries about wildlife.

How did you get started in the animal industry?

My father was a vet so I was always around animals as a child. From a very early age I wanted to be a vet because it seemed like such a perfect job. It's very challenging because there is so much to know about all the problems pets have and it's also very rewarding because people are very grateful when you make their pet better. I got involved in making TV programmes when the BBC wanted to make a documentary on veterinary students.

What is a typical week like?
Most weeks I spend working as a vet treating people's sick or injured pets. This involves talking to people about their animals, examining the pet and then deciding whether to treat with medicine or with surgery. Unlike a doctor, we have to do all aspects of the animal's treatment including X-rays, anaesthetics and surgery. When I am away filming my week basically involves trying to get up close to a particular animal to tell the viewers about its life. This might involve diving in the sea to film seals or sharks, or climbing trees to film monkeys. It is very varied and hard work.

It's very challenging because there is so much to know about all the problems pets have and it's also very rewarding because people are very grateful when you make their pet better.

What are the highs and lows of your current job?
I have to work long hours and spend long periods away from home, but I also get to visit amazing places all over the world, working with some of the world's most incredible species.

What challenges did you have to overcome to enjoy your current role?
The biggest hurdle to face was passing all my exams. Getting into vet school is not easy, so you have to have

very good exam results for your GCSEs and A levels. Once in vet school you have to pass exams every year for five years!

Are there any drawbacks from being in the public eye?
Being in the public eye has been fine. People are generally very nice and complimentary about the programmes I have been involved with.

What would be the next step for somebody in your role?
Who knows? TV is such a fickle industry that you can never tell where you will be in a year's time. I spend more time doing vet work now and want to improve my veterinary skills by going on courses and reading books. There's always something new to learn.

What advice would you give someone starting out?
Work hard at school because the more knowledge you have the more opportunities you will have. You never know how important lessons can prove to be until much later in life. Never think it's too late to do something different. If you really want something, then you have to work for it!

What's the story?

The UK is famous for being a nation of animal lovers. A large proportion of the population now has pets and needs to spend money on them, from dog grooming to veterinary expenses. Collectively the UK animal health market is worth about £360 million a year. The total market for cat and dog food alone is currently worth £1.6 billion per annum.

At the same time people's interest in animal welfare has mushroomed. New charities have been formed focusing on the need to take measures to protect specific habitats or species, such as our seas or the otter.

There has also been an upsurge in entertainment and tourism linked to animals and wildlife. This has presented new opportunities for work in zoos, wildlife tourism and in a range of other workplaces.

Some professions working with animals and wildlife, however, are oversubscribed. Take RSPCA inspectors, for example: there are over 2000 applicants a year for only 20 jobs. However, for some other types of jobs there is a real shortage of suitably qualified people, presenting an ideal opportunity for people who can target such professions. Wildlife survey skills, for example, fall into this category –

there are too few new people available to fill the posts that exist now, not to mention those that may be created in the future.

TRAINING ROUTES AND PAY

Some jobs working with animals and wildlife do not require any specific qualifications – just bags of enthusiasm and commitment. But for a growing number of jobs in this sector, qualifications of one sort or another are needed. Education and training opportunities include GCSEs, A levels, HNDs, National Vocational Qualifications (NVQs) and apprenticeships, as well as higher-level qualifications such as degrees.

DID YOU KNOW?

At present there are 323 uniformed RSPCA inspectors and 146 animal collection officers in England and Wales.

Pay rates are very variable, but in general you should not expect to get paid large amounts of money for working with animals and wildlife. The following is a rough guide to the range of wages on offer in this sector (remember that pay rates can vary in different areas and with different employers):

- A groom in a small stables can earn £10,000 a year
- A nature reserve warden can earn £15,000 a year
- An experienced veterinary nurse can earn upwards of £18,000 a year
- An established ecologist working for a government agency can earn £23,000 a year
- A junior university lecturer can earn £25,000 a year
- A vet with experience in a large practice can earn upwards of £35,000 a year.

Despite the old-fashioned stereotypes, employment prospects for men and women are good in all aspects of the sector. In jobs that were previously dominated by men, women are now catching up. The only barriers that remain are, therefore, in people's minds.

VOLUNTEERING

Many people find that in order to launch their career working with animals or wildlife they need to begin by doing some unpaid voluntary work. This is especially the case in those jobs which are very competitive to get into – such as being an RSPCA inspector. To begin with you need to be prepared to carry out fairly basic duties, such as administration tasks or answering the telephone, or practical work such as clearing scrub or digging ponds. Slowly, as you gain more experience, you may be offered more senior volunteering positions, such as working at public events or getting involved in the day to day running of the charity in other ways. Most charities actually rely on the work of volunteers, and you are often treated much the same as salaried employees, with access to useful training courses. This all helps you to gain valuable work experience which will in turn help you to find full-time employment.

You can learn more about specific volunteering opportunities in your local area by visiting the BBC's Breathing Places website (www.breathingplaces.org/public) and entering your postcode or home town. Find out about the opportunities in your local area to help out at a charity or other organisation which has links to the aspects of work you are interested in. It could be your first rung on the career ladder.

3

SALLY MILLS

Case study 1

NATURE RESERVE SITE MANAGER

Sally Mills works as the site manager at Ham Wall RSPB reserve near Glastonbury, Somerset, an internationally important wetland. The 190-hectare reserve has been created out of worked-out peat diggings to form a patchwork of pools and reed beds that attract a range of birds and other wildlife.

What's a typical day like?

The most exciting part of my job is that no two days are ever the same, so a typical day is quite difficult to describe. However, tasks that could make up a spring/summer day may be:

- Getting up at dawn to carry out a bird survey recording the breeding birds on the reserve
- Fuelling and starting the generator to aerate the new ecopod composting scheme that we are currently running, which aims to convert cut reed and grass into compost

Volunteering is a great way to get involved in this type of work and to gain experience of different management techniques and habitats.

- Checking the animals (we currently have three water buffalo and 17 highland cattle, which we need to count and check every day to ensure that they're all present and healthy)
- Getting back to the office to deal with any emails and administration, such as putting together budgets, planning applications, replying to enquiries and preparing for talks, meetings etc
- Going to see the contractor working for us undertaking wetland restoration. His work may involve putting in ground elevation levels with a theodolite so that he can re-profile the ground to the required heights needed for the establishment of different wetland habitats
- Liaising with staff and volunteers about work coming up
- If I haven't got up at dawn for a bird survey, then I might carry out practical work on the reserve, such as estate work (eg putting up gates or fences), creation work (eg planting reeds) or management work (eg cutting and removing vegetation).

When did you first become interested in wildlife?
Birds have dominated my life really, and have a lot to answer for! As an adolescent they were an endless source of fascination. At college they got me into trouble for missing lectures. Over the years, they have drawn me to interesting places and to meet interesting people. Now they often make me a target of ridicule amongst my peers, especially my hockey team! But they're a way of life, and as site manager at Ham Wall, they've led me to my biggest challenge ever – the transformation of a peat-extracted landscape into a mosaic of wetland habitats. But they are worth it!

What species do you work with?

I don't work directly with birds, but I help to provide habitats for them – such as reed beds, open water, wet scrub and grassland. These habitats benefit a variety of species, including endangered wetland birds like the bittern, marsh harrier and bearded tit, and some of our rarer mammals like the water vole and otter. The habitat creation and management work that we undertake on the reserve provides areas not just for rare wetland wildlife, but also for more widespread species such as the barn owl, stonechat and roe deer, and for a wide range of invertebrates and small mammals.

Did you consider any other jobs?

When I first left university, I became a freelance bird artist and sculptor and so was self-employed. The RSPB has been my one and only employer and since working for them on their nature reserves I've never wanted to consider other types of jobs.

What hours do you work in an average week?

This is a difficult one! My contract is written so that I will work the hours necessary to undertake the job – so I always work at least 9 hours per day. I regularly work 10-hour days and sometimes it can be as much as 12 hours. Lunchtime and

DID YOU KNOW?

Research is underway to try to discover why the house sparrow is disappearing from many of our gardens. The sparrow is now almost extinct in the centre of many UK cities, but we are still no closer to understanding why this is the case. The Independent newspaper has offered a reward for the first scientist to put forward a convincing reason for its decline.

coffee breaks only take place if I'm working with volunteers – otherwise, I work right through. I work at least one Sunday in a month, sometimes more – and getting that time off 'in lieu' (in place of the extra days worked) often never happens. Life is busy and there's always plenty to do.

After working on short-term contracts for the RSPB, I was offered a training post for three years, which involved working on three different reserves and studying for a Postgraduate Diploma (PgDip) in Environmental Conservation.

What training do you have?

I graduated in 1989, with a First Class BA (Hons) degree in Art. Then, after working on short-term contracts for the RSPB, I was offered a training post for three years, which involved working on three different reserves and studying for a Postgraduate Diploma (PgDip) in Environmental Conservation. This diploma involved all aspects of conservation work, including everything from practical skills like tractor driving, chainsaw operation and constructing boardwalks to academic skills like writing a management plan and conducting surveys. I was on short-term contracts for the RSPB for five years before securing my current permanent position, and this contract system was an excellent form of training. It enabled me to work on various reserves, gaining varied experience of different habitats and management methods, and acquiring a variety of skills such as dealing with the public, taking school groups and running events.

What advice would you give somebody interested in pursuing a career in this field?
You need to have a sound interest in the area in which you choose to work, and not be frightened of hard work and long hours. (However, the rewards are fantastic and well worth all the effort.) Volunteering is a great way to get involved in this type of work and to gain experience of different management techniques and habitats. In fact, when applying for jobs it's pretty much essential to be able to include volunteering on your CV, as it helps to illustrate your commitment to conservation. It's a great field to get involved in, but it's a difficult one to find work in, with lots of competition. Often the defining factor will be the range of interests you have and the variety of experience you've managed to obtain.

> ## DID YOU KNOW?
>
> The UK supports some of the finest estuaries in Europe, which are home to a wealth of rare and threatened wildlife. The reason for the estuaries' importance is the huge amount of invertebrates that lives in the mud — this is eaten by tens of thousands of birds.

What are the highs and lows of the job?
There are always highs and lows in any job. The lows are the amount of work to do and often the lack of resources to do it, the biting insects, the long hours and the reality of the bigger picture. The highs are seeing the reserve on a frosty, sunny morning, watching wildlife use areas that we have designed, created or managed, hearing the first bittern boom in a section of reed we established, watching the first wheelchair user test out the recycled plastic boardwalk that we installed, introducing grazing animals and seeing them venture into the reed bed, initiating new

projects like composting, obtaining the relevant permissions and gaining funding for a big project, and getting a big task completed with the volunteers.

What plans do you have for the future?
To remain in conservation work for the RSPB and hopefully to stay working at grass roots level, probably on reserves, because that's what I enjoy doing most. To continue to try and make a difference, but to increase the scale, to influence people and to try to get nature conservation even higher on the list of priorities.

4

What jobs are available?

This chapter provides an overview of the wide range of occupations that you can consider if you are interested in working with animals or wildlife. As explained in the introduction, the occupations in this book are divided up into six broad categories – but in reality there is some overlap between these categories.

ANIMAL HEALTH AND WELFARE

The animal health and welfare area is a very important part of the overall animal and wildlife sector. While a vets' practice may first come to mind, don't forget that there are many other jobs that fall into the category of animal health and welfare. They include animal behaviourists who work with problem pets, and dog wardens who round up strays from the streets.

Jobs linked to animal health and welfare are very varied and call for people working at a basic level right up to senior staff taking major decisions. Jobs available in this area include:

● Alternative therapist (working with sick animals using treatments such as homeopathy)

- Animal behaviourist (helping animals overcome problem behaviours)
- Animal technician (caring for animals involved in research)
- Dog beautician (pampering pets)
- Dog warden (rounding up stray dogs and helping to find them a home)
- Physiotherapist (helping animals overcome illness or problems with their movements)
- Vet
- Veterinary nurse.

DID YOU KNOW?

The leading bird holiday company Birdquest offers specialist birdwatching holidays to all seven continents. It employs professional ornithologists whose job it is to find as many species as possible for their wealthy clients.

If animal health and welfare is the career route you go down, you will need to be sympathetic and sensitive to the feelings of others as you will often be dealing with people who are distressed (because their animals are injured or sick).

You will need to be sympathetic and sensitive to the feelings of others as you will often be dealing with people who are distressed.

ANIMAL CARE CHARITIES

There are many charities doing excellent work to care for animals and to find them a safe home, with some well-known examples being Cats Protection (CP) and the Dogs Trust. Jobs available in this area include:

- Looking after animals in a rescue centre as a veterinary nurse or animal carer
- Training animals so that they can become good pets
- Working with the public to educate people about pets
- Carrying out administrative or other office-based tasks such as fundraising to help run the charity
- Going out and about to find and save injured animals.

A job working with animal charities is bound to put you in contact with people, so good interpersonal and communication skills are essential. It is also worth noting that work of this type is often quite poorly paid, so it is not an area to go into if money really matters to you.

Enthusiasm, commitment and lots of initiative are needed for all jobs working with animals and wildlife.

WILDLIFE MANAGEMENT AND CONSERVATION

This is a big growth area, with extra government money being ploughed into environmental schemes. More and more charities are working to safeguard threatened habitats and species, with grants from the National Lottery and other sources helping to boost their cause.

If you are interested in working in wildlife management and conservation, then there are two main routes to go down:

- Hands-on work managing habitats and working with particular animals. Jobs available in this area include nature reserve warden, gamekeeper, nature conservation species officer, fisheries consultant, wildlife surveyor and farm wildlife adviser

● More 'hands-off' work, which includes an increased element of office work and meetings. This could mean working with the public as an education officer, being an ecology researcher or working for a government agency.

The box below gives you an idea of the range of jobs available in a large wildlife conservation charity.

TEN JOBS WITH CONSERVATION CHARITIES

● **Database coordinator** – using IT skills to manage a large computer database on threatened species.

● **Director of conservation** – making important decisions about the conservation policy of the charity

● **Events coordinator** – ensuring that events are well organised and properly publicised

● **Field teacher** – working with children at nature reserves to help them learn more about birds

● **Fundraising officer** – working to raise funds so that the charity can continue its work

● **Magazine/newsletter editor** – coordinating the production of publications for members of the charity

● **Membership officer** – looking after the needs of members, including sending out membership cards and keeping them informed of new developments

● **Plant surveyor** – carrying out counts and making observations of birds on reserves

● **Special projects officer** – working on a particular project

or campaign that responds to the rapidly changing world of conservation
- **Warden** – being in charge of a nature reserve and carrying out management to make it better for wildlife.

THE ANIMAL AND WILDLIFE BUSINESS

The animal business in the UK is a multi-million pound industry. There is a huge range of possible jobs to consider – from horse racing to fish farming, zoos to wildlife tourism. If you are a budding entrepreneur, this is the area to focus on, with opportunities for new businesses to sell products and services. Jobs available in this area include:

- Animal breeder or trainer (including the breeding of show dogs, cats and other animals)
- Auctioneer
- Falconer
- Farmer and fish farmer
- Kennels and cattery work
- Riding instructor and work in a horse stud (where horses are bred)
- River bailiff
- Wildlife entertainment and tourism work (including being a bird tour leader, working in angling tourism, being a specialist animal park worker or even having your own insect road show)

DID YOU KNOW?

Dogs can be trained to sniff out all manner of dangerous substances and drugs. The dogs are trained to think of their work as a game, and are rewarded when they find what they're looking for. Dogs are playing a major part in controlling the international drugs trade at airports and ferry ports.

- Wildlife film-maker, writer or photographer
- Work with racehorses (including groomer, horse trainer and even jockey)
- Zoo work (including zookeeper, management roles and work with the public in an education capacity).

The jobs above are very diverse and require a variety of skills and levels of training. Not everyone is comfortable making money from animals, so you need to make sure you are happy with this concept before going any further.

SERVICES PROVIDED THROUGH ANIMALS

One of the wonders of animals is that, through their senses or by their sheer presence, they can really help people. Working with animals in this intimate way requires you to be very comfortable living and working with them. Some people seem to have a natural affinity with animals, and these are the people who would be most at home helping to provide such services as those listed below:

- Anybody who has seen a dog at work that has been specially trained to help blind or deaf people will never forget it. Animals can genuinely change, and even save, lives.
- Security concerns in recent years have meant that we often see sniffer dogs on our TV screens that are trained to root out explosives or drugs. Dogs also play a vital role in finding people trapped in buildings following natural disasters.
- Dogs are also being used in schools to improve children's behaviour, and trials are taking place with dogs that might be able to 'sniff out' the first signs of illness in some people.

- The 'pat a pet' service is a scheme where patients' pets are taken into hospital to help their owners to recover from illness.

INDIRECT ANIMAL AND WILDLIFE OCCUPATIONS

The final category deals with jobs that have a clear link to animals, but are somewhat removed from those listed above. Into this category fall examples such as animal nutrition experts, who design special menus for sick animals or those that require specific diets. People working in shops such as tack shops or feed merchants also work in indirect animal occupations. There are also various education-related jobs that fall into this category, such as teaching people about animal conservation in college or university.

SUMMARY

The summary table on pages 32–3 highlights key information about the range of jobs available working with animals and wildlife. For each category of job, there is a specific example given to illustrate the qualifications required, skills/attributes needed and likely starting salaries. Enthusiasm, commitment and lots of initiative are needed for all jobs working with animals and wildlife.

FINDING OUT MORE

When you are ready to carry out more research about a specific job, get in touch with employers. Many provide very helpful information packs that give much more specific detail about what the jobs are like than is possible here. Websites are also a key source of up-to-date information, with useful ones listed in the further information section at the end of this book.

Category of job	Examples	Specific example	Relevant qualifications (highest level listed)	Skills/attributes needed	Approximate annual starting salary
Animal health and welfare	veterinary work, physiotherapist, animal behaviourist, dog warden, alternative therapist, animal technician	Veterinary nurse *Note:* *minimum age for enrolment 17*	4/5 GCSEs at A*-C including English language, maths and a physical or biological science, foundation diploma	Interpersonal skills, communication skills, empathy, ability to work in a team	£9500
Animal care charities	rescue centres worker, charity jobs	RSPCA inspector *Note:* *minimum age for enrolment 22*	GCSEs in English language and science, Higher diploma	Compassion for animals, confidence, communication skills, ability to manage confrontation	£17,000
Wildlife management and conservation	scientific researcher, gamekeeper, ecologist, farm wildlife adviser, marine biologist, fisheries officer	Biodiversity officer	Degree in ecology or environmental science or related area	Field identification skills, computer skills, communication skills, report writing skills, influencing skills, data management skills	£19,000

Category	Examples	Job	Qualifications	Skills	Salary
The animal and wildlife business	farmer, fish farmer, auctioneer, work with racehorses, riding instructor, horse stud, river bailiff, animal breeder or trainer, kennels and cattery worker, zoos, falconer, wildlife entertainment and tourism	Zookeeper	No specific qualifications needed (on-the-job training provided), but many applicants have done animal care courses	Respect for animals, good communication skills, physical fitness	£10,500
Services provided through animals	dog handler for police or customs, mounted police	Dog handler	No specific qualifications needed (on-the-job training provided), but many applicants have done animal care courses	Affinity with animals, communication skills, confidence	£12,500
Indirect animal occupations	animal nutrition, working in a pet food shop, tack shop or feed merchants, education	Tack shop owner	No specific qualifications needed, but good business sense is important	Business and enterprise skills, communication skills, specialist knowledge of subject	Depends on success of business – sometimes very little on start up

5

Real lives

STELLA HIGHAM

Stella Higham is a vet working in a four-vet first-opinion small animal practice, based in Barnard Castle, County Durham.

What is a typical day like?

Busy! We spend a lot of time in the consulting room, dealing with appointments for anything from vaccinations to euthanasia. Routine operations, such as neutering, are done in the morning. Each day, a variable number of animals requiring emergency care and operations are admitted. We regularly see cats that have been hit by cars, dogs that have eaten a stone or toy that needs to be removed and animals requiring a caesarean operation. Often the day is followed by working the night on call.

When did you decide that you wanted to be a vet?

Around the time that I had to choose my A levels, after enjoying work experience at vets, stables, farms and kennels.

The job can be extremely rewarding and interesting.

Did you consider any other jobs?
Yes, I was interested in other science-related jobs.

What are the advantages and disadvantages of working as a vet?
The advantages are that the job can be extremely rewarding and interesting. The disadvantages are the long working hours and it can be stressful at times, as people usually have very strong emotional attachment to their pets.

What do you enjoy most about your job?
The successful treatment of a very sick animal.

What personal qualities do you think are important for the job?
An interest in veterinary medicine and therefore the motivation to work the long hours and investigate cases well. Also good communication skills, empathy, patience, an ability to stay calm under pressure and good observational skills.

What are your plans for the future?
I plan to choose an area of veterinary medicine that I am particularly interested in, and specialise in this. There are a number of certificates that vets can work towards, whilst working, to achieve this.

KAYLEIGH MCINTYRE – TRAINEE VETERINARY NURSE

For those interested in a career within a vets' practice, then it is not a lost cause if you're not academic enough to get the grades to become a vet. Veterinary nursing is an alternative career route to consider, and it is now possible to study this subject to degree level at university. To find out more about this important role, we interviewed Kayleigh McIntyre, who is a trainee veterinary nurse at the Dalehead Veterinary Group.

What's a typical day like?

A rota is done each week so what we do on the various days is decided beforehand. The days include:

- Kennel days
- 'Admits' (admit and discharge for operations) and puppy and kitten clinics
- 'Op days', where the nurses assist with surgical procedures and X-rays
- 'Lates' which are days when we have to stay for evening surgery which finishes at 7.00pm.

Today is a kennel day, starting at 8.00am. The first half-hour is spent cleaning kennels, giving medication, checking drips, feeding and then writing up each dog's records. From 8.30am until 9.00am we do the kennel rounds where every 'in-patient' is discussed – what has to be done with them, whether they're going home or not, etc.

At 9.00am the veterinary nurse on admit brings through the animals that are having operations and our job is to weigh them. This morning I assisted with a dog dental that involved extracting some teeth and a clean and polish. Nurses can clean and polish, but aren't able to do any other procedures.

Next there was a dog with a wound that had to be resutured. 'Suturing' is the technical name for stitching a wound. Some more serious wounds need these stitches to be replaced every so often, or occasionally stitches drop out, and the stitches are put in again in a process known as 'resuturing'. After the resuturing, we gave a rabbit a tear duct flush. Lunchtimes vary, as they are staggered between the nurses working to ensure that there's a nurse supervising animals recovering from anaesthetics at all times.

In the afternoon the kennels are swept and mopped, drips are checked and the dogs are fed. I then do any lab work that needs doing, which could include running through samples or doing urine tests. Finally any animals that need discharging are discharged and I ensure that all relevant owners have been telephoned.

Finishing times are variable from 4.30pm onwards, but they're not guaranteed. Sometimes I work overtime if, for example, an emergency comes in.

When did you first become interested in animals?
At the age of 3.

When did you decide to do veterinary nursing?
When I left school after doing my GCSEs.

Did you consider any other jobs?
Yes, I did consider doing equine physiotherapy and I would like to have been a vet if I had got the grades.

What training have you had?
At the moment I'm doing a pre-vet nursing course (which is designed for people who don't have the appropriate GCSEs), and to do this you need to be a working at a vets' practice. I've also done a National Diploma in Animal Care.

Is the work what you expected it to be?
Yes – and more.

What hours do you do in a typical week?
32 hours plus overtime (which I can either be paid for or take as time off in lieu).

What plans do you have for the future?
I hope to become a fully qualified small animal nurse and fully qualified equine veterinary nurse.

Work hard and show that you can apply yourself to any situation.

What are the highs and lows of the job?
The highs of the job are working with very ill animals and seeing them go home 100% recovered, especially when you haven't expected them to survive. The lows of the job are when animals come in that have to be put to sleep.

Do salary levels reflect the work that you have to do?
Not at all.

What advice would you give someone interested in pursuing a career in this field?
The best thing that you can do is to get as much work experience as possible, and try to get any work placements you do at a veterinary surgery. Work hard and show that you can apply yourself to any situation.

GAVIN CLUNIE – ANIMAL CARER

*Looking after animals in a zoo or safari park often comes
high on the wish list of people wanting to work in this area.
Gavin Clunie, who features in the next interview, works as
an animal carer in the rhino section at the South Lakes
Wild Animal Park in Dalton-in-Furness. He has worked
there for approximately two years, but prior to this worked
as a crisis journalist in war-torn countries.*

What's a typical day like?
I start my day at 8.00am. On arrival at work the first stop
is the 'brew room' where we have a cup of tea or coffee
and a quick chat to share information with other members
of staff about the current happenings around the park. I
then check every single animal (at present I work in the
rhino section but I also care for the giraffes, baboons and
porcupines). Mucking out is the next job and this involves a
big dumper truck! I also make sure that the areas where
the public walk are clean and that the information boards
and signs are correct and ready for the visitors.

At 10.00am we have a keepers' meeting for about half an
hour (including another brew). During this time, I fill in the
welfare diary, where we write information on the animals –
for example noting details of mating cycles. This diary
ensures that every keeper is aware of all the welfare issues.

When the meeting has finished any jobs still to do are
completed and then I prepare food for the animals in my
section. Our lunch break is next and can be anywhere
between five minutes and half an hour – the time is not
guaranteed, as the animals do not work to a timetable!

Next job is the hay run and there can be up to 60 bales of hay to move. I then check that all the equipment is clean and ready for the next day. Planning ahead is important to ensure smooth running from day to day.

Then I have another brew before doing the giraffe talk for the public. Giraffes eat leaves in the boughs of trees, so after the talk I cut some off the trees around the park, and prepare breakfast for the other animals in my section ready for the morning.

Finally I go and get the animals in. This job can take five minutes or two hours. If it has been raining the rhinos love the mud pool in the bottom of the field, and are somewhat reluctant to come in! My day ends at 5.30pm or 7.30pm. I do work long hours in the summer, but in the winter when there aren't as many visitors I get some 'time back'. This is not a nine-to-five job.

Our lunch break can be anywhere between five minutes and half an hour — the time is not guaranteed, as the animals do not work to a timetable!

When did you first become interested in working with animals?
Previously I was a crisis journalist, and had no interest in zoo jobs. However, I had some experience of animals through my family, from having animals around. I got this job because I broke my ankle in a skiing accident and, while I was recuperating, I sent a few CVs out. I was asked to an interview at the park, and subsequently got this job. Looking back, I realise that I must have had some key

transferable skills from my previous jobs that gave me an advantage over other applicants.

What are the highs and lows of the job?
The lows of the job are always stinking of you know what! And it's hard work physically. The highs of the job are that it's so wonderful to be surrounded by so many different animals every day.

What training did you do?
The training was on the job. To begin with I shadowed other keepers for a week. Over the next 12 weeks I started to do things on my own. Some people who work here have animal management degrees, but the most important things are that you use common sense, are assertive and are prepared to work.

What personal qualities do you think are important for the job?
You need to be outgoing and confident. I also have to do talks and am surrounded by the general public, so tolerance is a useful quality. The rest you learn as you're going along.

JENNY HOLDEN – OWL CHARITY CONSERVATION OFFICER
Some people's ambition is to work with wild animals rather than those in captivity. This is a dream that has been realised by Jenny Holden, who is a conservation officer for the World Owl Trust based at Muncaster Castle, Cumbria. In this interview she tells us more about her role.

What's a typical day like?
Normally I start work at 8.00am, but today it was 6.00am, because, at the moment, I'm hand-rearing a badger and

two owls. On the way to work, I checked two barn owl nest sites and found that in one of the nests the eggs had hatched. Whilst I was at the sites I also collected some owl pellets.

At 9.30am I arrived at work and the day started with a group of school students. They met the owls and I did some pellet dissection with them. Next on the day's job list was checking letters and emails. We liaise with various other conservation organisations and government departments such as the Department for Environment, Food and Rural Affairs (DEFRA). I regularly attend shows with the birds to give talks, so I spent some time planning these.

Careful records are kept of all the nest sites in order to keep a check on the owl populations to see whether they are increasing or declining. After planning the talks, I continued to write up some of the results from last year. The records are computerised so, after visiting the nest sites, I enter the data into the computer, including details such as the number of chicks and eggs. If we can catch the parents, we put rings on their legs with identification numbers so they can be traced.

After this, I spent some time with the birds we use for the educational visits – Jimmy the eagle owl and Mia the short-eared owl. At 4.00pm I started to prepare for the Crick Boat Show this coming weekend, where I will be giving a couple of talks. Today my day will not finish until about 9.00pm because, when I leave work, I am going to a meeting with local farmers and DEFRA.

When did you first become interested in animals?
When I was 3 – I used to crawl around the garden picking up creepy crawlies! From the age of 7 I'd go out on to the wildlife reserves and, at age 11, I worked with a hill sheep farmer. When I was 14, I did my first zoo work experience and continued in this field working at Chester Zoo and, while at university, at London Zoo.

What animals do you work with?
I do a lot of work with owls, which are the top predators in the food chain. But I look at the whole food chain, so this includes butterfly and red squirrel conservation. I'm a licensed bat worker and do this in my spare time.

Did you consider any other jobs?
Not really, I always wanted to do this.

What hours do you work in an average week?
Officially 40 hours – unofficially, unlimited hours. I always have a tent in my car so that I can camp next to owl nest sites. I try to catch up on hours in the winter time when it tends to be quieter.

What training do you have?
I have a BSc in Biology and Media. I write for magazines and newspapers to supplement my income. I'm a licensed bird ringer as well as a bat worker.

What advice would you give somebody interested in pursuing a career in this field?
Get going – if you want to do well you need to get stuck in as soon as possible. The more you do with different species of animal the better. Wildlife Watch is a good

group to join (it's the junior arm of the wildlife trusts) as they give you the chance to meet reserve wardens, which helps you to make contacts. Some of the major zoos such as Chester Zoo have placement schemes for older students, which allow you to work with a keeper for a month. You need to gain as much experience as possible. There are hundreds of graduates out there and you need to stand out from the rest.

Wading through piles of smelly owl pellets is not much fun until you find something interesting like a bat skull ... then it's brilliant!

What are the highs and lows of the job?

The highs have to be the close encounters with wild animals or the discovery of a new nest site. I also find it very interesting when I find a pattern in the data. The lows would be having five school visits a week and answering the same questions over and over. Wading through piles of smelly owl pellets is not much fun until you find something interesting like a bat skull ... then it's brilliant!

What plans do you have for the future?

To start a PhD, then maybe move on to something more research-based. At the moment I'm happy to stay here and see the Owl Trust go forward. I may eventually go into broadcasting.

6

Tools of the trade

Many young people have a romantic notion that working with animals is exotic and glamorous. Some think that the work only takes place in picturesque locations, where the weather is glorious. But reading through the stories of people already working in this field should balance this image. Whilst there are definitely plenty of positives, there are inevitably some negatives too and these represent key challenges for anybody considering working in this sector.

This chapter considers what you will need to make a success of a career working with animals and wildlife. The range of jobs you can do is bewildering, so the particular skills you might need for the career you choose could be quite specific. Nevertheless, it is possible to summarise some of the main skills and qualities you will need whatever job you find in this sector.

- Spending all day working with animals can be physically and mentally exhausting. A degree of **determination, stamina** and **patience** is, therefore, essential for working in this sector.
- You need to have total **dedication** to your work because you may have to work long and sometimes

unsociable hours, with very little time off and minimum pay. These are not the kind of jobs people do 'just for the money'.

- It is very rarely a nine-to-five, Monday-to-Friday job. Sometimes you could be required to work evenings and weekends, so Saturday nights out are never guaranteed. Therefore **flexibility** is obligatory. But if you have a **passion** for what you're doing you can feel a great sense of achievement when things work out well.

- Good levels of **physical fitness** and **endurance** are required, particularly if you're working in a stable yard or at an animal park and have to muck out ten animals a day! After a week of this even the physically fit will be tired.

- Most jobs will involve working with both animals and the public so good **communication skills** are essential. Take, for example, a veterinary practice where communication between the general public and members of your team would be a daily occurrence.

- **Teamwork** is very frequently required, so you should be able to work effectively as part of a team as well as on your own. Knowing when to take the lead and when others need to take charge is important, as is identifying what you need to do to help your team achieve its goals.

- Animal behaviour is unpredictable so you have to demonstrate **confidence** and show who is boss. The odd bite or kick could still occur; this is something you will need to get used to!

- A strong but **unsentimental commitment** to animals is crucial because, quite frequently, upsetting situations do arise when an animal might die. You sometimes have to make difficult decisions that are in the interests of the

animal rather than designed to make you feel better.
- **Respect** and **compassion** for animals are important attributes as you'll be working with them on a daily basis. Remember that you are not going to be working with animals as pets, so you will need to develop a **professional** and **responsible attitude** to dealing with them.
- It is important **not to be squeamish** about animals' bodily functions or the sight of blood: if you are, then you will have to face up to these issues pretty soon if you are serious about working with animals or wildlife.

Some jobs are quite academic; others require practical skills while others need you to have a good business sense. It is therefore important to be clear about what particular skills and qualities are important in the job(s) you are most interested in. To do this you should talk to people already carrying out the job. Listen carefully to what they have to say and try to imagine yourself in the job on a day-to-day basis. If you start to have second thoughts then you might want to reconsider whether the job really is for you!

Quiz

This quiz is intended to help you find out how much you know about animals and wildlife. It will also allow you to consider some of the key issues about working in this sector.

WHAT DO YOU KNOW ABOUT WORKING WITH ANIMALS?

1 WWT stands for …

    A Wildfowl and Wetlands Trust
    B Whale Welfare Trust
    C World Waterbird Trust

2 If you were using a hand lens, what job could you be doing?
    A Identifying plants
    B Surveying birds
    C Studying the ecology of lichens

3 An aviary is …
    A A place where bees live
    B A duck's nest
    C A large cage or building where birds are kept

4 What does NFU stand for?
    A National Fisheries United
    B National Farmers' Union
    C Nature for Urbanisation

5 Which of the following are breeds of cat?
    A Ragdoll
    B Labradoodle
    C Maine Coon

6 An Arctic skua is….
    A A seal
    B A bird
    C A polar bear

7 A National Nature Reserve is ...
   A A site that protects an area of historic interest
   B A government-designated area of national importance
      for wildlife or geology
   C A site where rare animals are bred

8 A cattery is ...
   A A place where cats are treated
   B A place where cats are groomed
   C A place where cats are bred or looked after

9 What does BVNA stand for?
   A British Veterinary Numbering Association
   B British Vole Naming Association
   C British Veterinary Nursing Association

10 What does an ecologist do?
   A Studies snakes in captivity
   B Examines the relationship between the environment
      and actions that affect it
   C Works out the budget for wildlife areas

11 Which of the following is the UK nationally important for?
   A Breeding seabirds
   B Flamingos on migration
   C Wintering wading birds and ducks

Answers

1. A. The WWT (Wildfowl and Wetlands Trust, www.wwt.org.uk) is a charity working to safeguard wetlands for wildlife and people. It runs a network of reserves across the UK, including Martin Mere, where the BBC's Autumnwatch programme was based.

2. A and C. Hand lenses are small optical devices that are used to see fine details in close-up, typically magnifying up to x10 what the naked eye can see. They cannot be used for making distant objects appear closer.

3. C. An aviary is a large cage or building where birds are kept. Aviaries are used to keep birds in zoos, and in people's homes where birds are kept as pets.

4. B. The National Farmers' Union (www.nfuonline.com) is the organisation representing the interests of farmers and growers in the UK. The NFU's mission is to bring quality produce to the market, care for the countryside and care for the welfare of animals.

5. A. (Ragdoll) and C (Maine Coon) are both breeds of cat. The Maine Coon is a native American longhaired cat and is generally regarded as a native of the state of Maine. Ragdolls also originated in the USA and the breed first came to Britain in March 1981. The labradoodle is a breed of dog.

6. B. An Arctic skua is a seabird that can be seen in the Shetland and Orkney islands, and is often seen flying low and fast above the waves. They eat mainly fish, and some eggs and young birds. Britain supports internationally important numbers of seabirds such as Arctic skuas.

7.   B. National Nature Reserves (NNRs) were established to protect the most important areas of wildlife habitat and geological formations in the UK, and as places for scientific research. They are owned by the government nature conservation agencies (eg Natural England) or private landowners, and managed by these agencies or approved bodies such as the wildlife trusts.

8.   C. A cattery is a place where cats are bred or looked after. People often take their cats to a cattery for safe keeping when they go on holiday.

9.   C. The BVNA was established in 1965, and aims to promote animal health and welfare through the ongoing development of professional excellence in veterinary nursing.

10.   B. Ecologists are employed in a variety of organisations to carry out research or ensure that wildlife is protected. Actions that can affect the environment include rainfall, farming, pollution, temperature shifts and industrialisation.

11.   A and C. The UK has huge populations of breeding seabirds on its cliffs and in the winter its estuaries are teeming with waders and wildfowl from Russia and Scandinavia, which find food in abundance. The nearest wild flamingos live in France.

Now add up your score, and have a look at the box overleaf to see how you did.

- 0–3 answers correct: hard luck – read this book to find out more!
- 4–6 answers correct: not bad – but you should widen your knowledge.
- 7–9 answers correct: well done – you have good knowledge of this field.
- 10–11 answers correct: you're a superstar!

Don't worry if your score wasn't perfect – there's lots to learn in any profession.

HESKETH FARM PARK, YORKSHIRE

Case study 2

Hesketh Farm Park, situated on the Bolton Abbey estate in the Yorkshire Dales, is run by Chris and Sue Heseltine and is part of a modern working beef and sheep farm. The Heseltine family have farmed the 600 acre farm since 1926, but the farm park has only been in existence since May 2005. The farm park gives the visitor an opportunity to actually touch, feed and learn about the animals that live on the farm. During the spring there is sheep lambing and orphan lambs to bottle feed, calves to feed, pigs that love having their backs brushed, eggs to collect and guinea pig and rabbit handling. As well as all that, there is a huge indoor play area, comprising a giant sandpit, straw maize and pedal tractors. Outside there is also a play area, pond and picnic area, and visitors are able to join the tractor and trailer tour which gives even more of an insight into the happenings on the farm on the week of their visit.

We have found that the majority of our visitors are very pleasant and relish the opportunity to learn about farming and the countryside.

Have you always worked with animals?

Chris has farmed since leaving school and my family have always farmed so, yes we have always worked with animals.

What made you decide to change from everyday farming to opening a tourist attraction?

The main reason for diversifying into something else was because the Common Agricultural Policy reforms had been announced which highlighted that it was going to be really difficult to make a decent living from farming for the foreseeable future, especially for beef farming.

What is a typical day like?

A typical day during the open season begins at 6.00am when we feed, clean out and bed up all the animals, sweep up everywhere so that by the time our visitors start to arrive at 10.00am the whole place is immaculate. We then spend the day doing all the feeding and handling activities with the public and any schools or nurseries that may be booked in. We close at 5.00pm and then clean and sweep up once again.

What are the highs and lows of dealing with the general public?

Dealing with the public is very different from straightforward farming. The public have huge expectations now, hence the reason we are so concerned about hygiene and cleanliness. We have found that the majority of our visitors are very pleasant and relish the opportunity to learn about farming and the countryside. However, you will always get some miserable person for whom nothing seems to go right and whatever you do or say is never going to make them smile. Luckily we've only had three miserable visitors in three years – that's not bad going! One of the major changes that we have had to get used to is working in holiday time and at weekends, but we have just had to adjust life so that we do lots of things with our three children in the evening and during the winter months when we are closed.

What training have you done?
We have both been on various training courses. Chris had to attend a course on how to drive a tractor, even though he's been doing this since the age of 17! We've also done training in first aid, health and safety, risk assessments, food hygiene and specialist training for school visits.

What plans do you have for the future?
As far as the future goes, we have no definite plans as such, but after each season closes we always have a huge list of things that need improving or amending and we never stop thinking about new things and attractions. We may be out somewhere and then see a good idea that could be adapted to our farm park situation.

Challenges to consider

Working with animals and wildlife can be one of the most satisfying of jobs, but it can also be one of the most challenging. This chapter considers the challenges it poses, which you need to bear in mind when considering working in this sector. If you haven't really thought deeply about what working in this sector would be like on a day-to-day basis, this chapter might serve as a wake-up call for you.

LONG AND UNSOCIABLE HOURS

As you will have seen from the Case studies and Real lives chapters in this book, those people who work with animals and wildlife often mention the unsociable hours that accompany the job. As animals are not very good at keeping to diary schedules, you should expect to work erratic hours, often getting up at the crack of dawn or staying late into the evening.

This makes it difficult to have a normal social life, and means that your friends and loved ones need to be really understanding of your situation. Unfortunately, these long hours are not necessarily reflected in the pay you receive, and overtime pay is not always provided. Instead, a flexible view is often taken, and you're expected to 'catch up' with your private time when things are less busy.

REAL-LIFE STORY: WATER, WATER EVERYWHERE

2007 was probably the wettest UK summer since records began in 1914. Heavy rain caused serious flooding in a number of places and has been devastating for the livelihoods of some farmers across the UK. John has a farm in the Yorkshire Dales, and has had a worrying few months.

He told us: 'Animals that would normally have lived outside during the summer months had to be kept in, which has affected us financially as it meant we had to buy extra feed. It also meant more muck, so more work! The animals have suffered with more hoof problems due to the damp, and there was the added complication of foot and mouth disease which meant we were not able to sell calves because of the ban on livestock movement. In addition, this winter will be hard because the cost of hay, straw, sugar beet (to name just a few) will be high as floods damaged many of the crops.'

HOSTILE WORKING CONDITIONS

You will undoubtedly need to be a hardy soul to put up with the tough working conditions associated with many jobs working with animals and wildlife. If you are somebody who hates getting cold and wet or hot and sweaty, then this is probably not a career for you.

Likewise, you may well encounter mud, blood, urine and animal dung at some point during your working week, so if you're squeamish about these things you will need to develop a tougher attitude pretty soon if you're going to survive!

Many jobs working in this sector also require you to work outside, often in remote, hostile locations for lengthy periods of time. Although it is unlikely that you will be asked to work alone in the wilderness, having a strong independent streak will be a distinct advantage.

HEALTH AND SAFETY ISSUES

Working with animals and wildlife has its fair share of health and safety risks. While it is not as dangerous as some professions (such as the armed forces), you should be aware that cuts, bruises and occasionally more serious incidents will happen from time to time.

Animals can be unpredictable and you should not take it personally if they bite or kick you occasionally. For this reason you are not likely to enjoy working in this sector if you are fussy about getting the odd splinter, cut or bruise.

Animals can be unpredictable and you should not take it personally if they bite or kick you occasionally.

Bear in mind also that you will need a good level of physical fitness for many jobs working with animals and wildlife. A certain amount of basic strength will come in useful if you're handling animals, especially the larger ones.

EMOTIONAL ENGAGEMENT

There is no getting away from the fact that working with animals and wildlife can be emotionally draining. Despite trying to maintain a professional attitude to your work, it is easy to get attached to animals and it is sometimes necessary to make difficult life and death decisions that are hard to come to terms with.

This presents a key challenge for anyone considering working in this field. Although over time you will become more accustomed to making these difficult decisions, it will never be easy.

REAL-LIFE STORY: A PAINFUL DECISION

Working as an equine veterinary nurse can be a very rewarding job, but there are times when it is tough. It was late one evening and we were just finishing when an emergency came in. A pony emerged from a trailer, completely covered in weeping sores. I had never seen anything quite like it. I held him, while the vet took samples to test. This pony was clearly very poorly and would require intensive nursing over the next few days. Spending so much time with this pony meant I became quite attached to him. When the test results came back a few days later they were not good. The pony was suffering from a very rare disease and there was no way he would ever recover. The owners were informed and the painful decision was made to put him to sleep. As I led him out of the stable, I had a lump in my throat and tears welled in my eyes. We all knew that this was the right decision, as attempting to keep him alive with powerful drugs would only have prolonged a miserable life.

Training

9

One thing is certain about a career working with animals and wildlife – there is no single entry route in terms of qualifications and training. The range of professions is so wide: some require study to degree or even postgraduate level; others allow you to train on the job, having obtained a basic school education. A few don't even ask for any qualifications, just a willingness to learn new skills as you work.

ASK YOURSELF SOME KEY QUESTIONS

Before beginning to think about the different training routes for specific jobs, it is a good idea to sit down and have a long think about some basic questions:

- What qualifications are you currently studying for?
- What choices await you in terms of the qualifications that you can take?
- Are you the kind of person who prefers hands-on training on the job or studying at school, college or university?
- Do you have what it takes to get the grades needed to go to college or university to follow a specific course?
- Would you have the staying power to stick at a three- or five-year training course?
- Do you like courses that are focused on a particular job (vocational) or those that provide a broader education (academic)?

● Are you happy to take on the financial strain of studying full time? Many students leave college or university with large debts (£15,000 is not unusual).

In answering these questions you might like to talk things through with another person, for example one of your parents, a friend or a teacher. Whoever you do it with, it is vital to be totally honest about your capabilities and personal qualities. While there is no doubt that hard work and determination count for a lot, there is no use being unrealistic about what you can achieve academically.

Tens of thousands of young people considering a career working with animals and wildlife have their hearts set on becoming a vet, yet the number of students who graduate each year with a degree in veterinary science from UK universities is relatively small, with only a handful of universities offering courses. Competition for places is fierce, and you have to get very high grades at A level just to stand a chance of being offered a place on a course.

THE DIFFERENT PATHWAYS
The flowchart on the next page outlines a number of pathways into a career working with animals and wildlife. Because of the broad range of jobs available, you are sure to find a route that suits you. There are alternative routes that are worth bearing in mind too.

Many people study at university as 'mature students' (aged 21 or over), often on a part-time basis while working. It is perfectly possible to mix and match these qualifications at different times during your career. Your progression through your career is also likely to be marked by on-the-job qualifications and training at different levels, according to your particular interests and work demands.

Apprenticeships

There has been a large increase in the take-up of apprenticeships in recent years, and there are now over 180 to choose from across more than 80 industry sectors. Perhaps the reason why they have been so popular is that they provide you with the best of both worlds. They allow you to study for a nationally-recognised qualification and gain on-the-job training, while at the same time earning money. The fact that you gain valuable work experience is also a real bonus, since this is highly regarded by employers.

If you sign up for an apprenticeship you will need determination to succeed. You will have to commit yourself to at least one year of training and study, with some schemes asking you to sign up for two or even five years. You will also need to be able to switch from working one day to studying at college the next. A selection of apprenticeships linked to working with animals and wildlife is shown below, but note that new ones are being phased in all the time (visit www.apprenticeships.org.uk for more details):

- Agriculture, crops and livestock
- Animal care
- Environmental conservation
- Farriery
- The equine industry.

access to careers

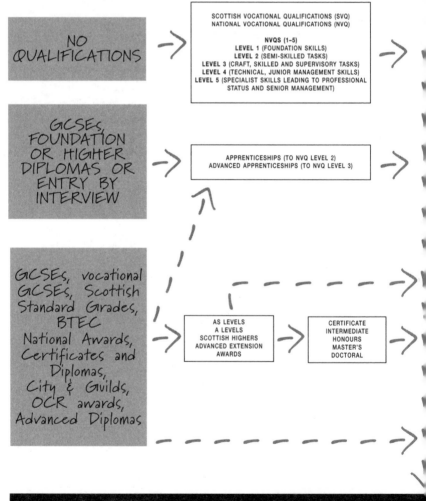

NO QUALIFICATIONS

SCOTTISH VOCATIONAL QUALIFICATIONS (SVQ)
NATIONAL VOCATIONAL QUALIFICATIONS (NVQ)

NVQS (1–5)
LEVEL 1 (FOUNDATION SKILLS)
LEVEL 2 (SEMI-SKILLED TASKS)
LEVEL 3 (CRAFT, SKILLED AND SUPERVISORY TASKS)
LEVEL 4 (TECHNICAL, JUNIOR MANAGEMENT SKILLS)
**LEVEL 5 (SPECIALIST SKILLS LEADING TO PROFESSIONAL
STATUS AND SENIOR MANAGEMENT)**

GCSEs, FOUNDATION OR HIGHER DIPLOMAS OR ENTRY BY INTERVIEW

APPRENTICESHIPS (TO NVQ LEVEL 2)
ADVANCED APPRENTICESHIPS (TO NVQ LEVEL 3)

GCSEs, vocational GCSEs, Scottish Standard Grades, BTEC National Awards, Certificates and Diplomas, City & Guilds, OCR awards, Advanced Diplomas

AS LEVELS
A LEVELS
SCOTTISH HIGHERS
ADVANCED EXTENSION
AWARDS

CERTIFICATE
INTERMEDIATE
HONOURS
MASTER'S
DOCTORAL

CAREER OPPORTUNITIES

NOTE: Mature students (aged 21 or over) often do not have to obtain as high examination grades as those going straight from school to unive

Apprenticeships are open-ended, allowing you to complete the course in your own time. Although they used to be aimed at young people, there is now no age limit for who can apply. To be accepted onto an apprenticeship you may need GCSEs in certain subjects; this will be dependent on the apprenticeship. You may also have to take some sort of test before being accepted, or perhaps an interview.

To get on to an apprenticeship you can approach an employer directly or apply through the Learning and Skills Council (www.lsc.gov.uk). For apprenticeships available outside England visit www.scottish-enterprise.com (Scotland), www.elwa.ac.uk (Wales) and www.delni.gov.uk (Northern Ireland).

Remember that getting accepted is like being offered any new job, and employers will only take you on if they think you are right for the job.

GCSEs and A levels

This is the traditional education route for most students in England, Wales and Northern Ireland, with Standard and Higher Grade equivalents in Scotland. In recent years vocational GCSEs have been introduced, which are qualifications linked to a specific job type. The new Advanced Extension Awards (AEAs) allow study beyond A level standard for high-flyers.

DIPLOMAS

The new Diplomas for 14- to 19-year-olds offer a mixture of classroom learning, creative thinking and hands-on experience. They are designed to prepare you for a range of careers and are available at three levels. A Diploma is an alternative to the traditional route of GCSEs and A levels, though in Years 10 and 11 you will still study subjects such as English, maths, science and PE. Diplomas look set to be a popular choice for those interested in working with animals and wildlife, as they are based around an area of work rather than traditional school subjects, and are very practical. They are also flexible in that you can go from doing a Diploma straight into a job, or into further study, then college or university. Of special interest to readers will be the Diploma in environmental and land-based studies, which is due to start in 2009 (see box). More background information on the new Diplomas can be obtained from www.direct.gov.uk/diplomas.

DIPLOMA IN ENVIRONMENTAL AND LAND-BASED STUDIES

This diploma has been developed to give you a good understanding of the 21st-century needs of businesses within this broad range of industries.

There are three levels of the Diploma:

Starting in Year 10 or above

- **Foundation Diploma** – a level 1 qualification taking about the same time to complete as four or five GCSEs

- **Higher Diploma** – a level 2 qualification taking about the same time to complete as five or six GCSEs

Starting in Year 12 or above

● **Advanced Diploma** – a level 3 qualification taking
  about the same time to complete as three A levels

You will complete a series of compulsory and optional
units all designed to give you knowledge, skills and
experience that will help equip you for life, learning
and work in the environmental and land-based field.

Compulsory topics will give a broad understanding of
the sectors and the way they interrelate. These topics,
which are organised under learning themes, introduce
you to productive and working environments, to plants
and animals, and the principles of developing a
sustainable environment. You have the flexibility to
choose from a wide range of additional or specialist
learning topics that are also part of the Diploma,
allowing you to tailor the course to your particular
interests. These include 'forests' and 'aquatic
environments' at foundation level and 'working with
animals' at higher and advanced level.

All students will also carry out a project to show the
skills and knowledge they have gained during the
course – this is of their own choice. Ten days' work
experience are also an important part of the course,
and give you the chance to learn and be mentored by
professionals in your chosen field.

More details of this Diploma can be obtained from
www.diplomaelbs.co.uk.

National Vocational Qualifications

The appearance in recent years of National Vocational Qualifications (NVQs) at five levels has allowed people to obtain work-based qualifications while doing a job. NVQs are open to people of all ages and abilities, and relate directly to the job you are carrying out. Scotland has its own version – the Scottish Vocational Qualifications (SVQs). NVQs mentioned below also exist as SVQs.

The five levels that can be obtained through NVQs are shown in the flow chart on page 64. The higher the number, the higher the level of specialisation and managerial duties you will be carrying out. NVQs are an indication of how well you carry out a particular task, and the knowledge and understanding you have to perform your job well. When working towards an NVQ you can be given credit for the skills you may have already gained through your experience carrying out a job.

NVQs are awarded in a wide range of sectors and by a variety of organisations, some of which also offer their own or other qualifications. Some of the awarding bodies which offer NVQs in working with animals are included below as examples, but there are many others.

British Horse Society

The British Horse Society (BHS) offers the following NVQs covering the full range of stable work:

- **Horse Care (level 1)** – you need to pass five foundation units, such as 'Assist with the care of horses' and 'Maintain health, safety and good working relations'. This level is a stepping stone for trainees. An extra accredited unit, 'Ride horses in an enclosed area', is available in addition.

- **Horse Care (level 2)** – you need to pass eight compulsory units, such as 'Prepare and provide non-ridden exercise and aftercare' and 'Load and unload horses under supervision', and one optional unit chosen from a wide selection including 'Assist with reproduction, parturition care and young stock' and 'Assist riders with special needs'. This is the basic qualification for horse work and should take about 18 months.

- **Horse Care and Management (level 3)** – you need to pass six compulsory units, such as 'Plan and monitor routine care' and 'Prepare horses for work', and an optional set of units covering one of exercising, schooling, light horse driving, heavy horses, trekking, polo, breaking, breeding, coaching and competition. Some extra accredited units are also available, such as 'Contribute to the management of stallions under supervision'.

> **DID YOU KNOW?**
>
> The PDSA's mission is to care for the animals of needy people, to provide vet care that is free to sick and injured pets, and to promote responsible pet ownership. Some 4650 animals are treated every working day.

The BHS also awards its own internationally recognised qualifications, sometimes known as **Stage Examinations**. Unlike NVQs, these are examined on specific dates at approved centres. The main qualifications run from Stage 1 to Stage 4, each of which is divided into Horse Care and Knowledge, and Riding. Each half can be taken separately, but both must be passed for the full qualification. Horse Knowledge and Care Stage 3 equates to the Groom's Certificate, while Horse Knowledge and Care Stage 4 is the Intermediate Stable Manager's Certificate. The Stage Examinations are primarily designed for teachers and future teachers, with Stage 3 onwards qualifying you as an International Instructor at different levels.

For more details about these and other awards, see www.bhs.org.uk.

BTEC National Qualifications

These are qualifications focusing on a specialist occupational area and leading into employment or higher education, now awarded by Edexcel. They can be taken at a variety of levels, the most well known being Nationals and Higher Nationals (see below). BTEC National Awards, Certificates and Diplomas are approximately equivalent to one, two or three A levels respectively, and the Diplomas are sometimes used as an alternative route of entry for students going to university. The BTEC Nationals available in Animal Management are as follows:

● **National Award** – you choose a route from Animal Rehabilitation, Exotics, Kennel and Cattery Management or Pet Store Management, and in each case take one core Business Management unit and five specialist units. Some of the units, such as Animal Health, are available in all streams. Others are specific to some or one, such as Wildlife Rehabilitation and Management, Aquatics

Management, Working with Cats and Dogs, and Breed
Development and Welfare.

- **National Certificate** – you choose either a general
  route, or Care or Science, and take five core units
  (including a Specialist Project Study) plus seven
  specialist ones. Some units are the same as those in the
  National Award, and some (such as Animal Behaviour
  and Animal Nursing) are available in all Certificate
  streams. Others are restricted to the general route and
  Care (such as Care and Welfare of Farm Livestock) or
  the general route and Science (such as Ecology and
  Conservation).

- **National Diploma** – you similarly choose from the
  general route, Care or Science, but take seven core
  units (including Industry Experience) and 11 optional
  units. There is only a small amount of variation in units
  available compared to the Certificate, except that you
  now have less room to avoid subjects you don't like!

Most units are assessed internally, with some of the core
units being marked externally. Similar ranges of qualifications
are available in Agriculture, Countryside Management, Fish
Management, Horse Management and other related areas.
For further details, check out www.edexcel.org.uk.

City & Guilds

City & Guilds is a leading provider of vocational qualifications
in the UK, and awards more than half of the NVQs. Its
qualifications assess skills that are of practical value in the
workplace, with over 500 different qualifications to choose

from. Jamie Oliver, Gary Rhodes and Alan Titchmarsh have all studied for City & Guilds qualifications earlier in their careers. City & Guilds is also closely linked with the apprenticeships scheme described earlier and there are several qualifications linked to a career working with animals and wildlife, such as veterinary care, dog grooming and animal care.

The **NVQ in Animal Care** is available from City & Guilds at levels 1 to 3. A general pathway is available at all levels, while at levels 2 and 3 you can specialise in Zoos/Wildlife Establishments, Dog Grooming, Pet Care and Retail, Boarding, Animal Welfare, Breeding and Open Farms and at level 3 a Dog/Animal Wardens route is available.

Other City & Guilds qualifications within animal care are Animal Care (levels 2 and 3), Dog Grooming (levels 2 and 3), Pet Store Management (level 3) and Veterinary Care (level 2). In most cases you have to take certain core units and then choose options. Find out more at www.cityandguilds.com.

Higher National Certificates and Diplomas

Higher National Certificates (HNCs) and Diplomas (HNDs) are approximately equivalent to one or two years of a degree. They allow study in an area that is closely related to a profession, such as countryside management or horse studies. You can study for an HNC or an HND in a wide range of subject areas, and these courses are ideal if you are not sure whether you want to commit to a degree course. There is the option to convert to a degree later if you wish to go down this route. The BTEC HNC in Animal Management consists of four core units (including Animal

Husbandry and Biological Principles) and six specialist units from a selection including Project Management for Land-based Industries, Biotechnology and Genetics, and Animal Law and Ethics.

Degree-level study and beyond
For some careers it is necessary to obtain degree-level qualifications. Most jobs that need a good scientific grasp of the subject matter fall into this category. Courses at this level now come in a wide range of types and levels, with the UCAS website being a goldmine of information on this education route (www.ucas.ac.uk). Traditionally the preserve of universities, degrees are now being offered by an increasing number of further education colleges too.

Foundation degrees
These may suit people wanting to study at university level while continuing their working life. Employers are involved in the design of these courses in collaboration with colleges and universities. This means that the courses are often available locally. Flexible study methods (eg distance learning, evening classes) ease the burden on those in work. They take two to four years to complete, depending on whether you study full or part time. There is also the option to continue for another period to complete an honours degree. With no set entry requirements and account taken of any previous experience in a job, these degrees are becoming more and more popular.

Honours degrees
Honours degrees, such as Bachelor of Arts or Bachelor of Science, are the most common degrees offered. They take from three to five years full time depending on the course

DID YOU KNOW?

The UK supports many rare breeds of sheep, cows and pigs, but some of these breeds have declined and are at risk of extinction. Specialist farmers are working to safeguard this animal heritage for future generations.

taken, and can also be taken part time or by flexible learning (or a mixture of the two). Many degrees are focused on a specific subject, rather than being pitched at a particular profession. As such they can offer a wide range of employment options if you are still undecided about a precise career.

Master's degrees and doctorates

These qualifications, which are only offered by universities, are the pinnacle of academic study. Master's degrees usually take one year full time and typically combine a taught element with a research project. They focus on a very specific area of study, which is sometimes closely related to a profession (eg wildlife management, animal health and welfare). Doctorates are a major undertaking, requiring at least three years of full-time study. They are mostly research-based, requiring you to carry out in-depth studies on a topic of your choice and write a 100,000 word thesis on your findings. Many people who do doctorates stay on at university to continue their research, as well as lecturing students.

GENERAL ADVICE

Other advice that will help you to decide on appropriate
entry routes for specific careers includes:

- Talk to people about what specific training courses or
  qualifications are like, but remember that they are giving
  their views and you might find things are different for
  you.
- Pay visits to colleges and universities to find out more
  about the courses and what student life is like there.
- Some courses offer sampler days that allow you to get a
  taste of the course without committing yourself.
- Read up about different training routes for specific
  careers, making sure you take advantage of websites,
  which often contain the most up-to-date information.
- Don't rush into any decisions; any course is a significant
  commitment and you need to be sure that you have
  made the right choice.

10

NICK HENDERSON

Case study 3

Nick Henderson is a falconer working at the Corio Raptor Care & Rehabilitation Centre near Lancaster.

How did you find yourself in your current job?

My interest in wildlife began in earnest when I became an RSPB warden in North Wales, working with the red kites in the early days when there were only 12 pairs. My current employer, Corio Raptor Care & Rehabilitation (www.raptor.org.uk), started up when the opportunity to help birds arose, and is still a small independently-run charity that specialises in the care and rehabilitation of birds of prey. We have been operating for 10 years and work extensively with the local police, RSPCA and veterinary practices. We take in many birds each year, and those assessed and considered suitable for being released are returned back to their natural habitat to be of benefit to the species.

To know you have really made a difference to a life through your own efforts and skill is reward enough

When did you first decide you wanted to work with animals?
During my school years, I knew that I wanted to work with animals, although at the time it was just helping at my local veterinary surgery.

How did you get started in the animal industry?
By accident, when someone brought an injured heron to me which I nursed back to health. The RSPCA contacted me and asked me to think about taking injured birds of prey in as well, as they were so impressed with how I managed to get the heron fit and well again.

What is a typical day like?
The first job is to get the birds out of their night quarters and check that all is well. Following that, I check the hospital birds and monitor the progress of the sick birds. Then I begin the task of cleaning out the night quarters, checking the aviary birds, and cleaning the aviaries, which are on a rota system. Next, I prepare the food for that day and individually feed the birds, then get food from the freezer (which can include chicks, mice, rats etc.) to defrost for the following day. Later we carry out administration work and if needed, make equipment for the birds such as leashes or blocks. Then, at the end of the day, the birds are placed back into the night quarters.

What are the highs and lows of the job?
The lows of the job are:

- The cruelty cases that we receive.
- The difficulty of having leisure time, plus the near impossibility of having holidays, due to the nature of the work involved, as you cannot just go away and leave the

birds with anyone, as they have to have knowledge and be confident in taking over from you.
- Raising money.

The highs of the job are

- When an injured bird starts to respond to treatment – it's as if they know you are trying to help them.
- The release of a bird is something special, especially if they have really fought to survive. It's a good feeling to know that it's you who has helped the bird to do that.
- When an imprinted bird comes in with a history of cruelty and neglect and they start to greet you with a call of recognition – that's a nice warm feeling to know that they have accepted and trust you.

There are many other highs to this job, far too numerous to mention, but to know that you have really made a difference to a life through your own efforts and skill is reward enough.

Did you have to do any training?
Not to begin with, as I used common sense and knowledge I gained from a good book. However, later I did attend first aid courses at London Zoo and British Wildlife rehabilitation courses, which were not available when I first started.

What personal qualities do you think are important for the job?
An ideal person needs to be dedicated, and have a keen interest in birds. They should have plenty of patience, a calm disposition, a gentle nature and not be too bothered about working alone. It would also be good to have

practical ability, as having to make all the equipment is essential.

What advice would you give somebody interested in pursuing a similar career?
First of all, do voluntary work for any animal welfare agency. It may also be useful to go to college and obtain qualifications in animal welfare and handling, and, if working with birds is the first choice, go to a specialist course where they teach husbandry. This includes learning about hygiene, dietary needs and general care of the bird, housing and hacking back (getting ready for release) and general first aid.

There are organisations that you can join to begin with, such as Raptor Rescue (www.raptorrescue.org.uk) which is a national rescue and rehabilitation group that teaches individuals how to set up and become rehabilitators.

Try being a volunteer at a large centre such as Monastery Castle (there are plenty of others) or at another rehabilitation centre to see if it is what you really want to do, as there is a less pleasant side to animal care eg plenty of cleaning up and of course, many casualties.

11

KAREN RUSHTON-WRIGHT

Case study 4

GROOM

Karen Rushton-Wright works as a groom at the Northern Equine Therapy Centre in Rathmell, North Yorkshire. The centre has a swimming pool for horses, plus a solarium and equine veterinary facilities. Karen has been working with horses for the last 12 years, since leaving school at the age of 16.

What's a typical day like?

My day starts at 8.00am when my colleague and I begin by mucking out on average 15 horses. The number of horses does vary depending on the season and the number of veterinary 'in-patients' there are. We then give the horses water and hay, before turning the older ones out into the fields.

At 9.00am it's our turn for breakfast. First job after breakfast is to work the racehorses. This involves either exercising them on the road or

I enjoy working as a groom because you don't have the responsibilitie you would have if you ran your own yard.

cantering them in the field. When we finish their exercise we untack them, then put their rugs back on.

The swimmers are next and they are put on the horse walker to warm up. This gives us a chance to 'skip out' their boxes (remove any droppings) before we swim them. After they've swum they dry off under the solarium before being rugged up and returned to their boxes. Most of the horses enjoy swimming, but occasionally you do get one who might dig his hooves in! The horses then get their lunchtime hay before we get our lunch at 1.00pm.

Most of the horses enjoy swimming, but occasionally you do get one who might dig his hooves in!

The afternoons are spent doing various jobs, including cleaning tack, sweeping and tidying up the yard. At 3.00pm we start to finish off. All the horses need skipping out, and fresh water and hay needs to be laid out. An average day will finish at 4.30pm.

At what age did you decide that you wanted to be a groom?
At the age of 4! I used to help out my mum's friend with her horses and have been involved with horses ever since.

What do you enjoy most about your job?
The fact that I'm getting paid to do my hobby. I couldn't afford to keep my own horse so this is the next best thing.

What qualifications do you have?
I left school at 16 and went to Craven College where I

completed my BTEC First Diploma in Horse Management, and the British Horse Society Stage 1 qualification. I then worked at the hunt kennels, a horse dealers and a stud before I came to work here at the Equine Therapy Centre.

What are your plans for the future?
I enjoy working as a groom because you don't have the responsibilities you would have if you ran your own yard. You get days off and the same kind of working conditions you get when you're employed in other jobs.

FAQs

There are many different jobs that involve working with animals and wildlife. So before deciding which career to choose, there are a number of questions that need to be carefully considered and answered.

WHAT ARE THE CAREER OPPORTUNITIES?

Employment prospects working with animals and wildlife are good, with strong growth in a number of specific areas in recent years, especially the environmental field. There are many different career options to consider, as outlined in the earlier sections of the book. For someone with the right attitudes and skills, there has never been a better time to go for a career working in this field.

WHAT ARE THE SALARIES LIKE?

Salaries vary tremendously between the various jobs. Generally not many jobs working with animals or wildlife pay high salaries, so you need to decide how important money is to you.

DO I NEED TRAINING?

That depends on which career you decide to choose. A number of jobs offer training once you have secured the job, but for others the training is intense and competition to gain admission to a course is high. One point that cannot be stressed enough is the importance of work experience. The more work experience you have, the better your chances will be. There are many people out there who

DID YOU KNOW?

Animals are thought to help people recover from illness and are also being used to improve children's behaviour at school. It is not known precisely how animals can affect people in these positive ways, but animals do seem to be able to help lower people's stress levels.

have university degrees, so when going for an interview, you need to be able to stand out from the rest. Start getting some experience as soon as you can, even if it means helping out at your local stables once a week or walking dogs for a kennel.

CAN I WORK ABROAD?

There are excellent prospects if you get the travel bug and want to work abroad. The animals and wildlife sector is on the up in many European countries, as well as in the USA, Canada, New Zealand and Australia. There are special rules that apply to working in other countries, so if this is something you are seriously considering, it is best to check with the employment authorities in the country concerned.

Opportunities also exist in less economically developed countries too, especially where large areas of wilderness survive, which support impressive populations of wild animals. However, in these countries pay is very low compared to that in the UK, and you might even be expected to work as a volunteer.

WHAT HOLIDAYS WILL I GET?

If you work for an employer there is a minimum holiday entitlement of 20 days' leave per year. Because of the nature of work with animals, bank holidays are not always guaranteed. If you are self-employed – as a farrier, for example – you need to plan the best time to take a holiday. This cannot be guaranteed in the summer.

WHAT HOURS WILL I BE EXPECTED TO WORK?

DID YOU KNOW?

There are 2000 dog grooming salons in the UK.

When working with animals and wildlife do not expect to be doing a nine-to-five job. Hours are often unpredictable and vary from day to day. In many jobs you will be expected to work your fair share of unsociable hours and these could be at the weekend. Crises can occur at any time and you might even be expected to be at work late into the evening. Breaks and lunches are not likely to be at set times either, as animals tend not to work to our timetables!

WILL I BE ABLE TO CHANGE CAREER IF I DO NOT ENJOY WHAT I AM DOING?

Once you have embarked on a course of study, it is always possible to change direction in your career. For example, the journalist interviewed on page 39 swapped reporting in war-torn countries for a job looking after rhinos. If you start a job working in one field related to animals or wildlife, this experience might enable you to work in another animal-related job, perhaps with a little more training. It would also count as valuable work experience in its own right.

WHAT ARE THE OPPORTUNITIES FOR RUNNING YOUR OWN BUSINESS?

The business opportunities are good as long as you can provide a product or service that is genuinely needed, or provides a new slant on an existing idea. To be successful in business you will need to be able to think creatively, be prepared to take risks and be willing to sell your ideas to others, not least the bank to secure a loan to get started!

There are many examples of people who have made a successful living through running their own businesses in the animal and wildlife sector. But there are also those whose businesses have failed. Despite the success of high-profile UK entrepreneurs such as Sir Richard Branson (the Virgin Group) and the late Anita Roddick (the Body Shop), starting your own business can be tough and success is far from guaranteed. Many self-employed people work longer hours than those working for an employer, and take home less pay. But the rewards and freedom of being self-employed are hard to put a price on.

The last word

After reading this book you should have a much clearer idea of what working with animals and wildlife is all about. You will also be able to judge whether such a career would suit you, although you may still be undecided.

There is a lot more to think about and do before you can finally commit yourself to this particular career route. You should try to follow the advice in the checklist below if you still feel committed to a career in this field:

- Be really clear about *why* you want to work in this field.
- Focus on a few specific job areas that really interest you.
- Discuss things with your parents or carers.
- Talk to as many people as possible who work with animals and wildlife.
- Listen carefully to what others tell you and be realistic about what you can do (but don't put yourself down!).
- Try to carry out some work experience as this is an excellent way of finding out what any job is really like and will make your job applications look stronger.
- Contact the organisations or companies that you are especially interested in working for to get further, more specific information.
- Discuss your options with a careers officer in a careers centre or at your school or college.

- Consider the entry options for your chosen career. Think about whether your existing skills, qualifications and experience will allow you to move into your chosen job area or whether new qualifications are needed.
- Decide whether you can afford to train full time or whether a part-time arrangement, allowing you to earn at the same time, is preferable. Some jobs may come with on-the-job training leading to a vocational qualification.
- Be determined; a lot is possible with a positive mental attitude!

Research is the key to effective decision-making.

Remember, research is the key to effective decision-making and you will find a wealth of organisations and help listed on the following pages that will help you make the right decisions.

Good luck with your career working with animals or wildlife!

THE LAST WORD

ARE YOU FIT AND ACTIVE?
☐ YES
☐ NO

DO YOU HAVE A PROFESSIONAL RESPECT FOR ANIMALS?
☐ YES
☐ NO

ARE YOU READY TO DEDICATE YOUR WORKING LIFE TO WORKING WITH ANIMALS?
☐ YES
☐ NO

ARE YOU READY FOR HARD WORK, OFTEN WITH LOW PAY?
☐ YES
☐ NO

ARE YOU PREPARED TO WORK UNSOCIABLE HOURS?
☐ YES
☐ NO

ARE YOU GOOD AT WORKING WITH OTHER PEOPLE?
☐ YES
☐ NO

ARE YOU ABLE TO WORK WELL WITH THE PUBLIC?
☐ YES
☐ NO

ARE YOU GOOD AT WORKING IN A TEAM?
☐ YES
☐ NO

ARE YOU SELF-MOTIVATED AND KEEN TO LEARN ON THE JOB?
☐ YES
☐ NO

If you answered 'YES' to all these questions then
CONGRATULATIONS! YOU'VE CHOSEN THE RIGHT CAREER!
If you answered 'NO' to any of these questions then this may not be the career for you

Further information

GENERAL CONTACTS

City & Guilds
1 Giltspur Street
London EC1A 9DD
Tel: 020 7294 2800
www.cityandguilds.com

Connexions
www.connexions.gov.uk

Connexions Direct (advisers)
Tel: 0808 001 3219
www.connexions-direct.com

Lantra
Lantra House
Stoneleigh Park
Nr Coventry
Warwickshire CV8 2LG
Tel: 024 7669 6996
www.lantra.co.uk

SORT IT OUT!

HOW DO I KNOW WHICH JOBS ARE RIGHT FOR ME?

No problem, you can log onto **cityandguilds.com/myperfectjob** and take 20 minutes to answer a range of online questions which looks at your interests, personality and lifestyle and suggests job areas which may suit you. Get all the information on job options, how to get started and where you can go to study.

cityandguilds.com/myperfectjob

Welsh Regional Office
Royal Welsh Showground
Llanelwedd
Builth Wells
Powys LD2 3WY
Tel: 01982 552646
www.lantra.co.uk/wales

Scottish Regional Office
Newlands
Scone
Perth PH2 6NL
Tel: 01738 553311
www.lantra.co.uk/scotland

National training organisation for the environmental and land-based sector.

The Careers Portal
www.careers-portal.co.uk

Award-winning online careers resource that is part of the National Grid for Learning, providing a gateway to careers and higher education on the web.

Remember too that search engines such as www.google.co.uk are an excellent way to find a whole range of additional information on job areas that interest you.

Considering a career with animals?

Have you got a vocational qualification such as a National Diploma, HND or NVQ level 3 in an animal related subject?

Maybe you have years of animal related work experience?

Then why not go to University?

Employers in the animal industries need skilled and knowledgeable staff, competent in issues such as animal welfare, legislation and nutrition. These staff need to have the communication skills to deal with the public, be confident in their own abilities, able to give presentations and to manage businesses. University can equip you with skills and knowledge to help you realise a fulfilling career in an increasingly competitive job market.

"VETNET LLN" is a lifelong learning network, which has been set up with government funding to help vocational students, like you, get onto a university course suited to your vocational qualification.

Visit our website www.vetnetlln.ac.uk and use our Courses in Animal and Veterinary Education tool (CAVE) to find out about courses near you.

CAREERS ADVICE AND INFORMATION

Learndirect
www.learndirect-advice.co.uk

UCAS ENQUIRIES
UCAS
PO Box 28
Cheltenham GL52 3LZ
Tel: 0870 112 2211
www.ucas.ac.uk

VETNET Lifelong Learning Network
National Office
Bletchley Park Science and Innovation Centre
Bletchley Park
Sherwood Drive
Bletchley MK3 6EB
Tel: 01908 363446
www.vetnetlln.ac.uk

ANIMAL HEALTH AND WELFARE

Getting into Veterinary School by Mario di Clemente
(Trotman, 2007)

British Veterinary Nursing Association
82 Greenway Business Centre
Harlow Business Park
Harlow
Essex CM19 5QE
Tel: 01279 408644
www.bvna.org.uk

Royal College of Veterinary Surgeons
Belgravia House
62–64 Horseferry Road
London SW1P 2AF
Tel: 020 7222 2001
www.rcvs.org.uk

**Royal Society for the Prevention of Cruelty to Animals
(RSPCA)**
Wilberforce Way
Southwater
Horsham
West Sussex RH13 9RS
Tel: 0870 333 5999
www.rspca.org.uk

ANIMAL CARE CHARITIES

Dogs Trust
17 Wakley Street
London EC1V 7RQ
Tel: 020 7837 0006
www.dogstrust.org.uk

Cats Protection
Tel: 0870 209 9099
www.cats.org.uk

People's Dispensary for Sick Animals (PDSA)
Whitechapel Way
Priorslee
Telford
Shropshire TF2 9PQ
Tel: 01952 290999
www.pdsa.org.uk

WILDLIFE MANAGEMENT AND CONSERVATION

British Trust for Conservation Volunteers (BTCV)
Sedum House
Mallard Way
Potteric Carr
Doncaster DN4 8DB
Tel: 01302 388888
www2.btcv.org.uk

Countryside Council for Wales
Maes y Ffynnon
Penrhosgarnedd
Bangor
Gwynedd LL57 2DW
Tel: 0845 130 6229
www.ccw.gov.uk

English Nature
Northminster House
Peterborough PE1 1UA
Tel: 01733 455000
www.english-nature.org.uk

Environment Agency
Rio House
Waterside Drive
Aztec West
Almondsbury
Bristol BS32 4UD
Tel: 01454 624400
www.environment-agency.gov.uk

National Gamekeepers' Organisation Charitable Trust
PO Box 3360
Stourbridge DY7 5YG
www.gamekeeperstrust.org.uk

National Trust
PO Box 39
Warrington WA5 7WD
Tel: 0870 458 4000
www.nationaltrust.org.uk

Natural England
Northminster House
Peterborough PE1 1UA
Tel: 0845 600 3078
www.naturalengland.org.uk

Royal Society for the Protection of Birds (RSPB)
The Lodge
Sandy
Bedfordshire SG19 2DL
Tel: 01767 680551
www.rspb.org.uk

Scottish Natural Heritage
Great Glen House
Leachkin Road
Inverness IV3 8NW
Tel: 01463 725000
www.snh.org.uk

The Wildlife Trusts
The Kiln
Waterside
Mather Road
Newark
Nottinghamshire NG24 1WT
Tel: 01636 677711
www.wildlifetrusts.org

World Wildlife Fund (WWF-UK)
Panda House
Weyside Park
Godalming
Surrey GU7 1XR
Tel: 01483 426444
www.wwf-uk.org

THE ANIMAL AND WILDLIFE BUSINESS

Association of British Riding Schools
Office No 2
Queens Chambers
38–40 Queen Street
Penzance TR18 4BH
Tel: 01736 369440
www.abrs-info.org

The Association of British Wild Animal Keepers
www.abwak.co.uk

British Dog Groomers' Association
Bedford Business Centre
170 Mile Road
Bedford MK42 9TW
Tel: 01234 273933
www.petcare.org.uk

Business Eye in Wales
Tel: 0845 796 9798
www.businesseye.org.uk

Business Gateway Scotland
Tel: 0845 609 6611
www.bgateway.com

British Horse Society
Stoneleigh Deer Park
Kenilworth
Warwickshire CV8 2XZ
Tel: 08701 202244
www.bhs.org.uk

Business Link
Tel: 0845 600 9006
www.businesslink.gov.uk

British Racing School
Snailwell Road
Newmarket
Suffolk CB8 7NU
Tel: 01638 665103
www.brs.org.uk

Farmers' Union of Wales
www.fuw.org.uk

The Farriers' Registration Council
Sefton House
Adam Court
Newark Road
Peterborough PE1 5PP
Tel: 01733 319911
www.farrier-reg.gov.uk

The Institute of Animal Technology
5 South Parade
Summertown
Oxford OX2 7JL
www.iat.org.uk

Institute of Fisheries Management
22 Rushworth Avenue
West Bridgford
Nottingham NG2 7LF
Tel: 0115 982 2317
www.ifm.org.uk

Invest Northern Ireland
Tel: 028 9023 9090
www.investni.com

The Jockey Club
42 Portman Square
London W1H 6EN
Tel: 020 7343 2236
www.thejockeyclub.co.uk

National Farmers' Union
Agriculture House
164 Shaftesbury Avenue
London WC2H 8HL
Tel: 020 7331 7200
www.nfuonline.com

National Farmers' Union Scotland
Rural Centre
West Mains
Ingliston
Midlothian EH28 8LT
Tel: 0131 472 4000
www.nfus.org.uk

SERVICES PROVIDED THROUGH ANIMALS

Guide Dogs for the Blind Association
Burghfield Common
Reading RG7 3YG
Tel: 0118 983 5555
www.guidedogs.org.uk

CVs AND INTERVIEWS

Winning CVs for first-time job hunters by Kath Houston
(Trotman, 2008)

Winning interviews for first-time job hunters by Kath
Houston (Trotman, 2008)

Winning job-hunting strategies for first-time job hunters by
Gary Woodward (Trotman, 2004)